The Universal Annuity System

The Universal Annuity System

Roger D. Cook

To order additional copies of this book, contact:
Xlibris Corporation
1-888-795-4274
www.Xlibris.com
Orders@Xlibris.com
84100

Contents

Chapter One

Utopian Thought

Every daring attempt to make a great change in existing conditions, every lofty vision of new possibilities for the human race, has been labeled Utopian.

—*Emma Goldman*

The word *Utopia* was first coined by Sir Thomas More. It represents an ideal society inhabited by men and women who reach dizzying heights of perfection, free from blemishes, and live in blissful harmony with each other. There is no war, poverty, stress, or misery in this perfect world. The men who conceived Utopias were visionaries who strongly criticized the times they lived in and found much wrong with it. They were men of immense courage who dared to criticize everything around them without fearing the consequences. Many of them could be considered geniuses gifted with intellectual originality and fertile imagination. Most of them were profound thinkers. However, these Utopians were out of touch with ground reality and were under the delusion that man could be perfect. They painted an ideal society, which seemed fantastic and was impossible to realize; nevertheless, they made immense contribution to philosophy and the history of social thought. They firmly believed that society could improve and the evils in them banished, and many of them deeply influenced their age.

Plato

One of the foremost Utopians was Plato. Plato was a giant of his times. His exact date of birth is unknown though most historians place the date of his birth around 428-427 BC. He was a student of Greek philosopher Socrates. A towering intellectual, he was a Greek philosopher and mathematician. Along with his famous student Aristotle, he laid the foundation of Western philosophy and science. He established the Academy, which became the most well-known school in the classical world. He left his mark on all subjects including philosophy, logic, rhetoric, and mathematics.

Plato's greatest work is *The Republic*—one of the most influential works that has left a deep impact on political theory and philosophy. It is totally original and has not been written with the help of his master. The exact date when the book appeared is unknown. Many scholars have placed the date around 380 BC. *The Republic* is in the form of a dialogue between Socrates and his friends about the nature of justice and an ideal city state. The title of the book is derived from Latin and means state or public matters. *The Republic* consists of ten books. In it, Plato outlines how an individual can lead a good and just life. Socrates used to speak ideas that are Plato's. Plato's republic is an ideal state governed by ethical values to promote the welfare and happiness of all its citizens.

Plato tries to find out the reason behind why men behave in a just manner. One of his objectives is to define justice. He tries first to define social and political justice and then later moves on to the concept of individual justice. According to Plato's ideal society, there are three main classes of people. They can be classified as producers, warriors, and guardians or rulers. Craftsmen, farmers, painters, masons, carpenters, artisans, etc., come under producers. A just society is possible only if the relation between the three classes of people is right. Each has to perform the function allotted to that particular class and maintain the power equation between the different classes. Each person must perform the task allotted to him without interfering with the business of others. Justice means specialization in one's own field.

Plato next moves on to the concept of individual justice, which he feels is similar to political justice. According to Plato, the soul of the individual too can be divided into three parts. The soul too has a rational part, a spirited part, and an appetitive part. The rational part of the soul is forever searching for truth and gives us our philosophy. The spirited part gives rise to emotions like honor, anger, and indignation. The appetitive part of our soul gives rise to desires and craves for money above everything else. In a just individual, the rational part of the soul takes command, and the other parts follow its lead. According to Plato, each class of society is ruled by one part of the soul. Producers are ruled by appetitive part, and hence, they run after money; the spirits rule the warriors who cherish honor above everything else while the guardians are dominated by the rational part and, hence, strive for wisdom. The guardians, because of their wisdom, are capable of becoming philosopher kings who make ideal rulers. He portrays three allegories: the sun, the line, and the cave. He gives us his theory of forms. Plato feels that the world can be divided into two kingdoms—the visible like the sun, moon, plants, and everything that we can see; and the intelligible like goodness, bitterness, sweetness. Both these kingdoms exist in relation to each other. The forms are actually objects of knowledge, which can be perceived by the rational part of our souls. The philosophers come closest to perceiving the form of good from which other forms like knowledge, truth, and beauty come into being. Plato feels that philosophers can possess true knowledge and are the only just men inhabiting the earth as they are dominated by the rational part of their souls. He is the perfect foil to the unjust man or tyrant. The tyrant is restless, tortured, and unhappy whereas the philosopher is calm, happy, and untroubled. All three classes have their own perception of what should be a good life. The producer class loves money, the warrior class values honor above all else while the philosopher class values truth the most. Plato feels that only philosophers can make good rulers and guide other people who should follow the philosopher's lead. Justice is connected to the form of good and enables people to live in peace and harmony.

He also lays great stress on education, which will not only impart knowledge, but also enable men to lead a virtuous and just life. Both boys and girls can receive education. Plato feels vices and diseases are caused by ignorance and can be banished with the help of education, which will develop not only the mind, but the body as well. Besides reading and writing, children are taught gymnastics, moral values, poetry, and music.

Thomas More

Another philosopher who made an immense contribution in the development of Utopian thought was Sir Thomas More. Born in 1478, Saint Thomas More was an English lawyer, social philosopher, author, and statesman. He has also been elevated to the position of a saint within the Catholic Church. He was also considered one of the foremost Renaissance Humanists.

In 1515, Thomas More penned his famous book *Utopia* in which he paints an ideal state. In fact, the word *Utopia* was created by More and means "no place." Utopia is an imaginary island whose people live happily in perfect harmony with each other.

Utopia starts with a written correspondence between Thomas More and other people, including Raphael who is the narrator of the book. These letters portray alphabet and poetry used in the island of Utopia. There is also a discussion on what is wrong with Europe, which has been torn apart by frequent wars and unrest. People live a miserable life there and yearn for better times. Raphael later discovers the island of Utopia and goes on to describe the lifestyle of the people living on the island. Life in Utopia is reasonable, orderly, and happy in contrast to the life people led in Europe. This imaginary island boasts of fifty-four towns with around six thousand households. Each household has ten to sixteen adults but the numbers change. Each town is governed by a mayor. The concept of private ownership is absent in Utopia. All goods are stored in warehouses. People can get what they need by requesting for it. The concept of buying and selling is absent. The citizens live in houses, but these are rotated between them after a decade. Life is safe and there is no need to lock doors. Agriculture is the primary occupation of people. Farming is known by all. Both men and women are expected to reside in the countryside and farm the land for a minimum period of two years. Besides farming, a person has to master another trade like weaving, carpentry, or masonry. Utopia does not know the problem of unemployment. Every able-bodied person is expected to work six hours every day. Simple garments are worn, and there are no fine apparels or dressmakers.

Slavery prevails in utopia. These slaves are from other countries or criminals. Each household has a couple of slaves. Criminals are tied with chains made from gold. The chamber pots too are made with gold. This is done so that people begin to dislike the glittering yellow metal. The community wealth is only used to trade with other countries. Slaves however can win their freedom by good behavior. Utopia has features of a welfare state like free hospitals. Divorce is permitted and priests can marry. However, premarital sex and adultery is punishable. Every meal is taken in the community dining hall. Various households are given the function of providing food to the people by rotation. People can travel within the island with the help of an internal passport. The island does away with the services of lawyers as the island has only simple laws that can be understood by all.

The island boasts of many religions like moon worshipers, sun worshipers, planet worshipers, ancestor worshipers, and monotheists. Religious toleration prevails, and all religions live in perfect harmony. Atheists, though allowed, are looked upon with suspicion. They can however reform by discussing their views with the priests of Utopia and change their ways. Raphael preached the gospel of Christ on the island, and many inhabitants of the island embraced Christianity. The position of women is subservient to men. Wives are governed by their husbands. Most women are allowed to perform only household tasks. A few widowed women are permitted to become priests. Compared to the women of their times, they enjoyed greater liberty and even receive training in warfare. However, women were supposed to confess their sins to their husbands every month. Gambling, astrology, hunting, and makeup were forbidden.

Francis Bacon

Francis Bacon too created his own Utopia. Born in 1561, Francis Bacon was a man of many parts. He was a statesman, scientist, lawyer, author, as well as philosopher. He was also appointed the lord chancellor of England. Bacon was honored with a knighthood in 1603.

In the year 1624, Bacon published a Utopian novel, *New Atlantis*. It was written in Latin, and in 1627, an English version appeared. In this novel, Bacon chalked out his ideal haven for mankind in a place where "generosity and enlightenment, dignity and splendor, piety and public spirit" rules. He also depicts his version of an ideal university, Solomon House, which bears certain similarities with a modern research university.

The crew of a European ship flounders as it loses its way in the Pacific Ocean near Peru. The crew then discovers the island of Bensalem. Once the travelers alight on the island, they are asked to leave by the natives. As they are unable to do, so they spend a few days isolated in the House of Strangers. They are then set free to explore the island and study its customs. The natives of the island practice Christianity even though they have very little contact with the outside world. The inhabitants of the island lead a secluded life hidden from the outside world even though they have immense knowledge of the world. As the travelers talk to the inhabitants of the island, they come to know the history of the island's origin and its customs like marriage and family. At the heart of the island is Solomon's House also called the College of Six Days Work. This is a state-sponsored scientific institution that boasts of trained investigators who collect data and conduct experiments. Gaining admission into this prestigious scientific institution is not easy. Only the most intelligent and best natives of the island can gain admission. In this house, scientific experiments are constantly conducted. One of the objectives of the scientists is to tame nature. The knowledge gained out of these experiments would be used for the welfare of society. Rapid advancement is made in the field of surgery, meteorology, and machinery. Bacon writes, "For the several employments and offices of our fellows, we have twelve that sail into foreign countries under the names of other nations (for our own we conceal), who bring us the books and abstracts, and patterns of experiments of all other parts. These we call merchants of light.

"We have three that collect the experiments which are in all books. These we call depredators.

"We have three that collect the experiments of all mechanical arts, and also of liberal sciences, and also of practices which are not brought into arts. These we call mystery-men.

"We have three that try new experiments, such as themselves think good. These we call pioneers or miners."

Unlike most philosophers like Plato, Bacon feels that human beings need not curb their desires. The advancement of science will make it possible to provide all kinds of material things that human beings could want and they can lead a luxurious life. Solomon House is Bacon's dream of a place where free intellectual growth is possible without any shackles. Bacon's vision is said to have inspired the creation of the British Royal Society.

Tommaso Campanella

We come now to an Italian Utopian. Tommaso Campanella came into the world in the year 1568 in the province of Reggio di Calabria. He hailed from a poor family. His father was an illiterate cobbler. A gifted child, he managed to enter the Dominican Order before he had completed fifteen years of his life. Here he studied theology and philosophy.

His most famous work is the *City of the Sun*. The title refers to a fictional island of Taprobane situated in the Indian Ocean right on the equator; hence, its name.

The book is in the form of a poetical dialogue between "a grandmaster of the Knights Hospitaller and a Genoese sea captain." His objective was to portray a model society that lived in perfect harmony with nature. He felt that the times he lived in was plagued by violence and injustice, and a change was desperately needed. The ideal city is on the slope of a hill and is protected by seven circles of walls. According to Campanella, in this city, every occupation is considered dignified. Even those who do manual labor are considered at par with rulers. Right from their childhood, people are made familiar with all kinds of work, but they later specialize in what they can do best. The island has no servants. A person has to work only for four hours a day on this island but nobody is idle. There are no possessions in this island. There is no money, and nothing is ever bought or sold. Food, houses, education, and even women and children are common to all. There are no families. Officials are appointed to monitor the fair distribution of everything.

The painted walls of the city are nothing less than an encyclopedia of knowledge. They contain all possible images of both arts and science. They contain pictures of planets, stars, heaven, minerals, vegetables, plants, arts, inventions, religious leaders like Moses, Jesus, and details of all countries. Knowledge is thus not kept hidden in books but in open display on the walls for all to see. According to Campanella, visualization makes learning easier and interesting. The community of wives is the most controversial feature of the island. Campanella separates sex from love. He feels men should breed like horses are bred so that the new generation that will be brought into the world will have first-class qualities. He advocated the scientific breeding of men. Love between men and women can be expressed in the form of friendship, mutual affection, and by exchanging gifts.

The religion followed in this island takes elements from Christianity. However, the citizens follow a religion which is close to nature. Citizens worship in an open temple. There are twenty-four priests in the temple who watch the stars and guide human beings in their affairs. Campanella dreamt of a world united, completely at peace, and ruled by a theocratic monarch.

Thomas Hobbes

Another great Utopian was Thomas Hobbes. Thomas Hobbes was an English philosopher who arrived in this world in 1588 in the city of London. Though he had an unhappy childhood, he graduated from the University of Oxford. In the year 1651, Hobbes penned his world famous work *Leviathan*. *Leviathan* went a long way in laying the foundation of Western political philosophy.

When Hobbes wrote *Leviathan*, the English civil war had ripped the nation asunder. In his book, Hobbes pleads for a strong central government in order to end chaos. According to Hobbes, peace is possible if a commonwealth is established by social contract. His commonwealth is ruled by a sovereign who has absolute authority. Hobbes work can be divided into four books: *Of Man*, *Of Commonwealth*, *Of a Christian Commonwealth*, and *Of the Kingdom of Darkness*. Book I is the most important as it outlines Hobbes's philosophy. Hobbes feels that human nature can be derived from materialistic principles. Therefore, human nature is constantly in a state of unrest and wishes to wage a war against each other. Naturally, peace is desirable, and the only way of achieving peace is to build a Leviathan or commonwealth through the principle of social contract. The social contract can be achieved by people. One person can say, "I authorize and give up my right of governing myself to this man or to this assembly of men on this condition, that thou give up thy right to him and authorize all his actions in like manner." The sovereign is bestowed with absolute authority. The social contract is permanent and cannot be violated. The government, once formed, cannot be changed. The sovereign is formed because most of the people want him to govern. The people must abide by the sovereign who has the right to take any measure necessary for the preservation of peace and harmony among his subjects. He cannot be labeled unjust. He has the sole authority to appoint ministers and councilors and wage war with other nations. The people cannot rise in revolt against him or execute him. The sovereign along, with his ministers, proposes and enacts all civil laws including those concerned with property. The sovereign also has the power of reward and punishment.

According to Hobbes, three types of commonwealths are possible—monarchy, aristocracy, and democracy. He feels monarchy is the best form of government. The question of succession will be decided by the ruler himself.

James Harrington

Another important utopian thinker of the era was James Harrington. His life spanned from 1611 to 1677. He was a renowned English political theorist. He hailed from an old family. He was a widely traveled man who visited Netherlands, Denmark, Germany, France, and Italy. His work *The Commonwealth of Oceana* brought him both fame and notoriety. He portrayed a Utopia and poured forth his political philosophy.

According to him, the need of the hour was a stable government. He felt unstable governments led to anarchy and were the root cause of all wars. He wanted to make an ideal constitution that would ensure stability. Harrington was in favor of a republican system of government in which people had a say. He said that "reason which is the interest of mankind, or of the whole," is "a law of nature" and described "the public interest of a commonwealth" as "nearest that of mankind." According to Harrington, it was possible to form a stable government only with the help of those who possessed landed property. Harrington wanted a commonwealth where every person who held land property would have a share in governance. However, Harrington was also not in favor of a few individuals owning large tracts of property. He felt that laws were needed to limit the amount of wealth an individual could possess. Men owning property would elect a senate. One of the duties of the senate was to make laws. These laws could come into force only after being ratified by the people. An elected magistracy was responsible for executing the laws. Elected officials could serve only for a limited period so that other citizens of the commonwealth also got an opportunity to have a say in the governing body. The society was bonded together with common interests. He laid emphasis on an "equal agrarian law" that monitored the distribution of property so that there was a balance of interests in the governing body. Harrington stressed on separation of powers, division of legislature, and the concept of rotation in men who held high offices. According to Harrington's Utopia, one third of the officials sitting in the senate are forced to leave every year through the power of ballot, and they may not be reelected for a period of three years. He also created a character named Olphaus Megaletor who was a generous lawgiver and who bore a remarkable resemblance to Oliver Cromwell. An angry lord protector Oliver Cromwell refused to allow the book to be published. Harrington was able to publish it only after appeasing Oliver Cromwell and convincing him about his good intentions.

Robert Owen

The French and Industrial revolution brought a sea change in the lives of people. In the initial years of the Industrial Revolution, the miseries of people increased. Into this world came Robert Owen who wanted to bring about change and was one of the greatest social Utopists. In 1771, in a small town of Newton in Wales, Robert Owen came into this world. He was one of the greatest social reformers of his time and is considered to be one of the founders of socialism. He received education only until the age of ten. After his marriage, he became the owner of New Lanark mills. Here he experimented with social reform. He refused to employ anyone below the age of ten and tried to shorten the working hours. He took a keen interest in the living conditions of the workers. He constructed new houses for them and paved the streets. He even opened a free village school. He also tried to improve their moral standards.

Robert Owen was also a philosopher. In his essays entitled *A New View of Society*, he aired his thoughts. He believed that the world and its inhabitants could not be categorized into good and bad. Men were molded by their circumstances. If the circumstances around a human being change, it is bound to bring about a change in his or her character. He dreamt of a new millennium where there would be no crime, misery, hunger, and violence. Owen felt much of human misery was due to frequent wars. He made an in-depth study of the causes leading to wars. He felt the major reason behind human suffering was the fact that human beings were forced to compete against machinery. He felt that man could be happy if they acted united against machinery. Owen's Utopia consisted of community life. He visualized around twelve hundred people living together in a huge building with a common kitchen. Families were to live in private apartments within the building. Children were to remain with their parents until the age of three, and then they will be brought up by the community. However, their natural parents could meet them at appropriate times. The community needed to be supervised by officials who monitored all their activities. Agriculture is the primary occupation. However, machinery does not lag behind. Owen feels that every community should possess high-quality machinery and provide a variety of employment opportunities. Owen also feels the necessity of every community being a self-contained unit.

In the beginning, Owen spoke out against conventional religion. He felt it was hypocritical. He wrote, "All religions are based on the same ridiculous imagination, that make man a weak, imbecile animal; a furious bigot and fanatic; or a miserable hypocrite." He wanted to reform the church. He also felt religious fanaticism is responsible for most wars. However, he believed in religious toleration. He felt man must prove himself by helping others. Owen understood the importance of education and wanted education for all so that people lead a better life. He wrote, "The three lower rooms (in the Institute) will be thrown open for the use of the adult part of the population, who are to be provided with every accommodation requisite to enable them to read, write, account, sew or play, converse or walk about. Two evenings in the week will be appropriated to dancing and music, but on these occasions, every accommodation will be prepared for those who prefer to study or to follow any of the occupations pursued on the other evenings."

Karl Marx

One of the most important Utopian socialists in relatively modern times was Karl Marx. Born in 1818, Karl Marx is one of the leading philosophers of his time and his thoughts laid the foundation of communism. Besides being a German philosopher, Karl Marx was also a political economist, sociologist, and historian. His most famous book is *The Communist Manifesto* in which he penned the famous line, "The history of all hitherto existing society is the history of class struggles." Classes could be defined by their relation to the means of production.

The world witnessed rapid industrialization when Karl Marx grew up and watched the plight of workers. Capitalism ruled. According to Marx, history proved that feudalism has been replaced by capitalism. Marx felt that capitalism too would be replaced by socialism. His Utopia was a stateless and classless society. However, this ideal state could be achieved only after the world had witnessed a transitional period that he called the dictatorship of the proletariat. His clarion call to overthrow capitalism was "Workers of the world unite. You have nothing to lose but your chains."

Marx's sympathies lay with the working class. He felt that the capitalist system thrived on exploitation as it survived by gaining surplus value from its workers. Marx thought that a person should feel exploited if he does more labor than what is necessary in order to produce goods. Marx felt as one class of people, the capitalists, has full control over the means of production, they exploit the other classes of people. The worker enters into the capitalist's domain in order to get the necessities of life. He has no choice as the alternative is to face starvation. The worker feels alienated. He sells his power of labor but has no control over the things he produces. These products are sold at a profit by the capitalists. Marx coins the term *surplus value* to describe the difference in what the working class receives as payment for the goods it produces and the actual selling price of the goods in the market.

Marx called people who worked or sold their power of labor in order to get money to survive as proletarians. While capitalists or bourgeois are people who own land as well as technology to produce goods. Naturally, the proletarians are far larger in number than the capitalists. Capitalists, however, made huge profits and used them to reinvest and improve the technologies at their command. However, Marx felt that this would lead to a crisis at regular intervals. The profit earned by the capitalists will decrease with economic growth. Economic depression will hit nations once the rate of profit falls below a certain level. Depression will bring about a steep fall in the price of labor. The proletariat will become even poorer, paving the way for a revolution. Marx prophesized that the desperate proletariat will overthrow the capitalists and take control over the means of production. This will bring about equality as well as economic growth and prevent crisis. The dictatorship of the proletariat will follow. The communist slogan is "From each according to his ability, to each according to his needs." The transition from capitalism to communism may be peaceful or violent.

Chapter Two

The Failure of Communism

Communism doesn't work because people like to own stuff.

—Frank Zappa

The twentieth century was the beginning of a movement to upset the very nature of the capitalist economy. This self-proclaimed next step in the evolution of economics is known as communism. In 1917, Russia became a communist country through the October Revolution and before long, within only a few decades, China, North Korea, Vietnam, and Cuba were communist countries as well. For the second half of the century, the constant threat of nuclear war between communist and capitalist countries was an ever-present danger. For fifty years, people seriously worried about whether or not their home would be around the next day or if it would be destroyed in a massive nuclear attack. By the 1980s, roughly one-third of the human population on earth was under communist rule through various revolutions.

However, after the fall of the Soviet Union, communism collapsed around the world and only a few countries like Cuba, North Korea, Vietnam, and China remain communist. In many cases, like with China, communism has taken on various capitalist ideals.

Communism as a philosophy and an idealistic social reform is not a horrible thing. It is a social structure where the concept of class is abolished and property is controlled to ensure everyone gets an equal share. It is sharing at a countrywide level, and if done right, it can be a highly beneficial thing for the country. Karl Marx stated that communism would be the final stage in society, and it could only be achieved by a revolution by the working class to allow for the equal distribution of goods and services.

Under pure communism, in the Marxist sense, is a classless, stateless, and oppression-free society. Under this type of communism, every member of the society helps to make decisions on what is to be produced and what policies are to be pursued. This allows every member of the country to take part in the decision-making process to make it a success or a failure.

Due to Self-Interest

The problem is that communism has failed because it fails to take into account the self-interest of individuals. They neither want to make decisions, nor do they want to share everything. With communism, the good of the many outweigh the good of the one. This means that while you may want to accumulate property and possessions, the world of communism does not allow this. You are required to think of everyone before you think of yourself, and this goes directly against the concept of most human nature, which is self-interest.

There are various types of self-interest, but we all typically focus on ourselves and those around us before we focus on society as a whole. This is why communism failed because, in the end, everyone wants to help themselves before they help others.

Individualism is in direct contrast to communism. Essentially, individualism is the moral stance, philosophy, or outlook that stresses the moral worth of the individual. With self-interest or individualism, the individual is the focus. Many consider this to be the natural order of things. In nature, animals will typically look for benefit for themselves before they look for benefit of the group of animals as a whole. Others disagree that individualism is not the natural way because of the need to protect the species in order to protect the individual. However, these theories do not take into consideration the habit of male predators to eat the young of other males in order to ensure their own young get a better chance at survival. This is only self-interest and not conscious or deliberate thought in helping the species as a whole.

So applying this to communism, we see why the basic human need for self-interest caused communism as a whole to fall. Even looking at the very leaders of communism, we can see that they practiced self-interest while requiring the citizens to sacrifice their own self-interests for the greater good. For example, Joseph Stalin owned several homes that he stayed in that were decorated with high-priced items. This was clearly against the communist ideal that he supposedly upheld. Therefore, it was clear that communism would fail because no one within the country would put the country first.

In many ways, the distribution of wealth within communism could not be done without the ability of individuals to greatly sacrifice what they had. Friedrich Hayek, who wrote *The Road to Serfdom*, argued that the even distribution of wealth through nationalization could only be achieved by causing citizens of a country to lose their political, economic, and human rights. Control over means of production and distribution of wealth was necessary to ensure that self-interest did not take over, and this could only be done through coercion of the citizens to ensure they followed communism and not the principle of self-interest.

This is why so many communist countries turn into totalitarian regimes. The reason for this is because there needs to be absolute control in order to make citizens put the country first instead of their own interests. Since this seems to go against basic human nature, it was always doomed to fail. As well, any country that uses totalitarian policies is always doomed to fail as the people begin to rise up. Even when citizens rise up to bring down a communist or totalitarian country, they are doing it for their own self-interest. They want to live in a free country with capitalistic ideals so that they can pursue their own happiness. While this may be one of the better forms of self-interest, it is still self-interest.

As Winston Churchill once said,

> A socialist policy is abhorrent to the British ideas of freedom. Socialism is inseparably interwoven with totalitarianism and the object worship of the state. It will prescribe for every one where they are to work, what they are to work at, where they may go and what they may say. Socialism is an attack on the right to breathe freely. No socialist system can be established without a political police. They would have to fall back on some form of Gestapo, no doubt very humanely directed in the first instance.

Objectivists often criticize communism because it devalues the individual by making it the policy that individuals could not choose their own values. This is why objectivists reject the communist ideal of rejecting property rights. This is why communism never has high economic outputs because the country is unable to fully put the interests of the citizens behind, the betterment of the country rather than the betterment of themselves.

A perfect example of this is the fact that China and Vietnam both had very high rates of growth only after they introduced market reforms that allowed them to be more capitalistic in the 1970s and 1980s. In the process, by doing this, they were able to reduce poverty. China, while remaining a communist country but introducing capitalism, reduced its poverty level from 53 percent in 1980 to 8 percent in 2010.

Looking at various communist states and comparing them with their capitalist counterparts also show why communism was doomed to fail. They could not make enough money because of the lack of self-interest. People make money in capitalistic economies because they want to buy things; they are pushed by self-interest to do well so they can live better. This is not seen in communism, which is why it fails.

Here is an example of how one communist country was compared with other countries that were capitalistic. This shows the big divide that exists between growth and governmental policies.

After World War II, Germany was divided into east and west with the east being communist. Before the war, East Germany's productivity in 1936 was 90 percent of the productivity in West Germany. In 1954, after the war, the productivity of East Germany compared to West Germany had fallen to 60 percent. Comparing the productivity of East Germany to all of Western Europe, we see that the overall productivity of East Germany was only 67 percent in 1950 and 60 percent in 1989.

Chapter Three

Today's Capitalism's Evolution

Fact is Our Lord knew all about the power of money: He gave capitalism a tiny niche in His scheme of things, He gave it a chance, He even provided a first installment of funds. Can you beat that? It's so magnificent. God despises nothing. After all, if the deal had come off, Judas would probably have endowed sanatoriums, hospitals, public libraries, or laboratories.

—*Georges Bernanos*

Capitalism is the most common form of market system and ideology in the world. Nearly all the countries on earth practice some form of capitalism. *Capitalism* is defined as an economic system in which the means of production are owned privately while the supply, demand, distribution, price, and more are decided by private decisions and market forces. Profit is distributed to owners who invest in business, allowing those with more money to make more money.

The Beginning of Capitalism

Capitalism grew from mercantilism, which itself got its start around the Age of Discovery, between the sixteenth and eighteenth centuries. Many merchants were becoming overseas traders, and overseas trade was increasing at an incredible rate. Mercantilism is seen as the early form of modern capitalism, but long-distance, merchant-driven trade was seen as far back as 2000 BC as well as in the Roman Empire. When the Roman Empire collapsed, most of Europe was then controlled by feudal powers, which did not function well with the concept of capitalism and the free market. Through mercantilism, the concept of a state selling more goods than it imports was created so that foreigners would have to pay the difference in precious metals that were being bought and sold. It was the merchants who argued that only goods that could not be found in the home country should be imported from elsewhere.

From this, European merchants began to look at state-controlled monopolies as a way to get their profits from buying and selling their goods. Francis Bacon said that mercantilism existed to provide the opening of well-balanced trade, the cherishing of manufacturers, and the banishing of idleness while repressing waste and regulating prices. Medieval towns all over Europe began to latch onto this idea, and local guilds popped up to regulate the economy under mercantilism.

Beginning of Small Businesses

Capitalism had its true beginning in America. Hand in hand with the Industrial Revolution, America took the lead in advancing the capitalistic economy. America was the opportunity to start your own business. With little start-up cost, it was easy to get started. Labor was in great demand, and the economy was expanding. With knowledge and a few tools, it was easy to be a blacksmith, butcher, tavern owner, or many other business owners. It was a great opportunity for small businesses.

Adam Smith, who created the groundwork for understanding capitalism as we know it, saw four main points.

1. Self-interest was a driving force for good in the economy. The interplay between a self-interest buyer and a self-interest seller will keep the price of a good or service within a reasonable rate.
2. The decision of what to produce is in the hands of supply and demand. If you decide to offer a product or service, someone must be willing to purchase the said product or service.
3. Competition between buyers and between sellers helps to set a fair price for a product or service.
4. Private property, which includes wealth, should be at the will of the owner.

The principles of Adam Smith in *The Wealth of Nations* seemed like ideal concepts in a time of small businesses, fast economic expansion, and high labor demands; but they changed when the world changed.

Beginning of Big Business

Railroads are a prime example of how a small business model and the principles of Adam Smith cannot be counted on to run all businesses in an economy. In the early 1800s, railroads began as relatively small businesses running rail lines between several cities. It soon became obvious that every business that wanted to run rail lines between the same cities made it unfeasible and unprofitable. So one line was run between the cities. By the mid to late 1800s, railroads were in the hands of a few railroad barons.

In the twentieth century, the government began to regulate the railroad industry because of its monopolistic practices. The automobile began in the early twentieth century, giving the railroad competition in transporting people. But the path for big business had begun. Other businesses followed: automobiles, utilities, household machines such as refrigerators, and other consumer products.

Today, we see big business replacing small business everywhere. The local mom-and-pop grocery store is Walmart. The local barber is Great Clips. The local hardware store is Home Depot.

Small businesses' main goal was profits while big businesses' main goals are profits and power. Does big business represent an evil that must be rectified, or does big business simply take advantage of its characteristics than at its means?

Globalization

With the creation of the East India Company and the Dutch East India Company, capitalism in its modern form began to be created. These first global companies were created by their nation-states, which gave them colonial and expansionary powers. Merchants who used to do the trading themselves now began investing in capital in both companies in the hopes of getting some sort of return on investment in the future.

Globalization is the process by which regional economies, societies, and cultures have become integrated through a global network that consists of global trade, global transportation, and global communication. Capitalism has created a global economy that is deeply integrated through trade, foreign investment, capital flows, and migration as well as the increased spread of technology.

The first phase of globalization was the colonization of other continents by European powers from the sixteenth to nineteenth centuries. However, with World War I, the first phase of globalization crumbled; and many blamed globalization for World War I as well as for the Great Depression that followed just over ten years later.

After the World War II, it was not countries that pushed globalization, but multinational corporations that were based out of the United States and Europe. While globalization has helped many get out of poverty and helped technology spread across the world, the integration of globalization across the planet made countries dependent on each other. The process of globalization began before big business. Did big business just take advantage of the existing globalization?

Countries that are dependent on each other are less likely to go to war with each other. War between Europe and the United States or between European countries themselves is very unlikely due to globalization.

If big business through globalization were not around, war would be more prevalent. Technology would be hoarded to prevent other countries from gaining an advantage over others. And poverty would grip many more countries.

The following is a list of some arguments against big business:

1. Sweatshops

Sweatshops are considered a by-product of globalization and capitalism. Capitalization and globalization created sweatshops because it gives corporations the power to exploit resource-poor countries in the international market. If a country has little resources or physical products that can be mined from its own soil, corporations will go into these countries and use the poverty of the nation to its own advantage. Companies will take advantage of poor labor laws and low wage rates so that they can increase profits by paying people much less than what they deserve. Sweatshops are widely used by clothing manufacturers and shoe manufacturers, including Nike, which has long been criticized. Countries don't want to put an end to these practices because if labor laws change to make it harder for companies to exploit individuals, the companies will simply move to another country. The multinational companies are so powerful that even the United States will not go against them. Several bills have been proposed in Congress to stop exploitation of poor countries. One such bill, the Decent Working Conditions and Fair Competition Act, would have made it a legal responsibility of companies to respect human rights by not allowing the import, sale, or export of goods made in a sweatshop. Not surprisingly, this bill failed in Congress as companies and their interests make money off exploiting the poor. This is something capitalism has created, and it is one of the worst things that our world deals with.

2. Overconnectivity

Globalization has caused the world to be so interconnected that it has greatly altered how countries and companies conduct business. This has bad effects because when something happens in one country, it deeply affects another country. Such as the subprime mortgage crisis in the United States led to a global financial crisis that was the worst seen since the Great Depression.

3. Brain Drain

Globalization has led to richer countries taking talented individuals away from poorer countries. While this may seem good, it robs poorer countries of the people who could help the country out of its poor situation. In Africa, the brain drain costs the continent $4.1 billion in the employment of 150,000 professionals each year. India loses $10 billion per year as a result of Indian students going abroad for their higher studies.

4. Environmental Destruction

One of the worst things that capitalism has created is environmental destruction. Industrialization, as a result of globalization and capitalism, has led people away from an agrarian society and into one that is concerned primarily with profit at the expense of the environment. There are several examples of how capitalism has ravaged the environment and destroyed the livelihood of the people who depend on their local environment. Examples include the following:

- China, due to rapid capitalization, is the world's leading producer of harmful CO_2.
- Within the next ten years, the tropical rain forests in Indonesia will be completely gone due to logging by companies.
- Within the next thirteen to sixteen years, the tropical rain forests of Papua New Guinea will be gone for the same reason. Logging companies from China and Japan are the biggest culprits in Indonesia and Papua New Guinea.
- Without recycling, zinc will be used up by 2037, indium (for soldering) and hafnium (for making control rods for nuclear reactors) by 2017, and terbium (for making CDs) by 2012.
- Around the world, coastal habitats—rivers, lakes, and the oceans—are being heavily polluted by companies. Many people are dying of thirst around the world while multinational companies are diverting water to make things like soft drinks and bottled water.
- The BP Deepwater Horizon oil spill in the Gulf of Mexico in 2010.

5. Food Security

Since capitalization and globalization reared their heads, grain production has increased by roughly 250 percent while the population of the planet has grown by roughly five to six billion people over the past two hundred years. As a result, it is very difficult for countries to maintain food security; and roughly one billion people around the world are starving to death while in other countries people are dying from eating too much. Food reserves are at a fifty-year low while the world will need 50 percent more energy, food, and water by 2030. The world needs to produce 70 percent more food by 2050 to feed the additional 2.3 billion who will be born. This is because of globalization and capitalization. It is estimated that by 2048, the world will have run out of wild-caught seafood.

6. Spread of Disease

The rate of the flow of information, goods, and people has caused deadly diseases to spread across the planet. This was first seen in the fourteenth century when the Black Death killed 33 percent of Europe's population due to the spread of disease along trade routes. Infectious diseases can now spread easily due to globalization. An example of this is AIDS, which kills one million people a year in the United States and is the leading cause of death among African-American women.

7. Drugs

Globalization has allowed drugs to become a huge business. The global drug trade is estimated to have $320 billion in revenues each year. Around the world, there are more than fifty million users of heroin, cocaine, and other hard drugs.

8. Poor Countries Bear the Brunt

Globalization does increase free trade among countries, but it hurts countries trying to save their national markets. The main export of poor countries is agricultural goods, which is sad when people realize that in those same countries, people are starving in incredible numbers. Large countries will subsidize their farmers, which then lowers the market price for the poor farmer's crop.

9. Outsourcing

The low cost of offshore workers means many companies go overseas to have products made. While we have already addressed the fact that this leads to people being exploited in poor companies, but it also has a significant impact in the country where the company is based. The loss of the manufacturing sector in the United States has resulted in many people losing jobs and resulting in the loss of much of the middle class in some areas. With no middle class, it is not easy for people to get out of poverty in areas where companies have chosen to outsource rather than hire locally.

10. Poor Labor Unions

In the United States, cheap labor elsewhere has caused the weakening of labor unions in the United States. Since memberships are declining, unions are losing their power and therefore hold less power over corporations. Now, corporations in the United States can easily fire individuals, replace workers, and lower pay because unions lack any sort of power.

11. Child Labor

Corporations, thanks to globalization, will often use child labor even though it is illegal all over the world. An increase in labor demand in poor countries means more goods being produced by children and therefore causing an even greater demand for child labor. Many children in poor countries are forced to look for cash by salvaging garbage, cash cropping, quarrying, prostitution, and pornography as a result of capitalism.

12. Poor Distribution of Wealth

One of the biggest things caused by capitalism and globalization is the poor distribution of wealth. According to the United Nations, the following distribution of wealth is found on earth:

- The richest 20 percent of the world's citizens control 82.7 percent of the income.
- The second richest 20 percent of the world's citizens control 11.7 percent of the income.
- The third richest 20 percent of the world's citizens control 2.3 percent of the income.
- The fourth richest 20 percent of the world's citizens control 2.4 percent of the income.
- The poorest 20 percent of the world's population controls only .2 percent of the income.

13. Competition for Jobs

There is a huge competition for jobs now as the world moves toward a global marketplace. As a result, there are more and more workers who are competing for jobs between developing countries and developed

countries. Since the 1950s, outsourcing to other countries has increased dramatically because companies want to save money at the expense of workers in the Western world.

Now, workers in the United States have to compete for jobs with others in developing countries. The problem is that the workers in developing countries work for less so companies, who are only concerned with profits, choose to pay less to workers elsewhere.

14. At the Mercy of Corporations

Sadly, due to the current recession, more and more people are left without jobs, and that puts them at the mercy of corporations. People are willing to work for less, so companies pay them less. Rather than pay people what they deserve to be paid, companies under the capitalistic system choose to pay people as little as possible so that they can make as much as possible.

Conclusions

These arguments have some merit. But the immoral practices are not restricted to just big business. The problems that arise are not in big business but lies in the nature of man. The self-interest that Adam Smith talked about in *The Wealth of Nations* has an ugly side. If you have self-interest without being tempered by concern for others, then these types of problems will come to pass. With self-interest and a lack of concern for others, people in government, big business, or small business will abuse people and nature.

These poor business practices demonstrate that some rules and regulations must be in place to control abuse of power. This is the domain of government. Government must have a moral structure. In the United States, government has cuddled up to big business and has lacked the moral fortitude to set the rules and regulations or to enforce those that were created to maintain proper standards. The financial crisis of 2009 was partially due to the removal of curtain regulation. The BP oil spill in the Gulf of Mexico showed the close connection between big oil and the U.S. government's Minerals Management Service.

In many poor countries, the situation is worse. Many governments in poor countries have complete power to do as they please and not respond to the general public's concerns. The evil of big business lies in our nature. We should continue seeking a greater moral structure in our society but not by eliminating big business. Rather, we should seek ways to take advantage of the nature of big business.

Chapter Four

What Can Be Done?

A little rebellion now and then is a good thing and as necessary in the political world as storms in the physical.

—*Thomas Jefferson*

Clearly, capitalism in its present form is not working, but at the same time, communism doesn't work. With capitalism, people are able to own things, but the desire to own things causes some to have more money than other people while millions go without their basic needs. However, with communism, there is money distributed to everyone; but people want to own things, so they naturally go against the system. What is needed is a balance between the two, and to do that, a change needs to happen. How does that happen?

Violence

When people think about changing the world, they believe that it involves violent resistance. Yes, violent resistance has brought about change. The American Revolution ushered in the age of democracy. The French Revolution did the same for France while communism fell as a result of violent protests in many of the Soviet Union's satellite countries. However, is it right to use violence to bring in a new change for the world?

Those who are against capitalism, however, point out that capitalism itself is violent. Through private property, interest, profit, and trade, violence is used as a means of defending what capitalists want to protect. Capitalist economies, some argue, needs war to expand, and therefore, structural violence is used to prevent people from being able to meet their basic needs, thereby killing them. An excellent example of this is the fact that so many people die around the world from diseases that there are cures for. Malaria in Africa could be wiped out almost completely if only everyone had extremely inexpensive mosquito nets. However, millions live without mosquito nets and therefore end up dying of a preventable disease.

The problem with violence is that it is a double-edged sword. It cannot work because when you use violence to achieve something, you only end up hurting yourself. An excellent example of this is the French Revolution.

The French Revolution

The French Revolution began as a result of citizens no longer wanting to live under the rule of a king who did not care about them. They had heard what happened in America, and they wanted the same thing. So they revolted with extreme violence. Eventually, the king and queen were beheaded and France looked toward a brighter future. However, following the violent French Revolution, the Reign of Terror began as mass executions of enemies of the revolution began. Roughly sixteen thousand to forty thousand people were beheaded and killed over the course of only thirteen months during this dark period. Maximilien Robespierre found out the hard way that while you can change things with violence, that violence will come back to get you. After the fall of the monarchy, with no stable government, food riots began; and as a result, Robespierre became the ruler of France, essentially a dictator, and it was he who essentially began the Reign of Terror. He spoke that terror was necessary and inevitable and should be lauded because the French Republic could only exist by the virtue of its citizens and that terror was maintaining the republic, and therefore, it was good.

Eventually, people had enough of the man who preached violence to maintain the republic and he was beheaded on the guillotine in 1794, thereby ending the Reign of Terror.

Types of Revolution

Robespierre's Reign of Terror is an example that shows violence usually comes back to hurt you in some way or another.

As a result of the French Revolution, we often see any sort of revolution, even one to upend a horribly ineffective economic system, as violent. However, Alexis de Tocqueville, a classic scholar, reasoned that there were in fact three different types of revolutions that can happen.

The three types of revolutions are the following:

1. Political revolution—this is a revolution that is done politically by using political avenues and required laws to make a change.
2. Sudden/violent revolutions—this type of revolution involves the creation of a new political system, which can also transform an entire society. Often the lingering effects of a violent revolution are dictators, a loss of services, death of citizens, and more.
3. Slow transformation—this is the type of revolution that will completely change a society, but it will take several generations for it to be accomplished. Often this is a peaceful revolution that has little or no bloodshed and often has a longer-lasting effect than other types of revolutions.

In this book, we are not talking about violent revolution or change. Violence does not work, and who would the violence be against? Corporations? How do you hit a corporation? Plus, if you use any sort of violence against a corporation, you will most likely end up in jail as most of the lawmakers and political leaders work for corporations in one way or another across the world these days.

Nonviolent Resistance

No, what is needed is a combination of the first and second forms of revolution, the political and slow transformation. Think nonviolent resistance can't work? Well, there are several examples throughout history that say it can. Nonviolent resistance is essentially the practice of achieving a socio-political goal through protests, noncooperation, and civil disobedience. Many great individuals have used nonviolent resistance as a way of creating change including Leo Tolstoy, Mahatma Gandhi, Andrei Sakharov, Martin Luther King, and Lech Walesa. Between 1966 and 1999, nonviolent resistance helped play a vital role in fifty of the sixty-seven transitions from authoritative government. Some examples from the twentieth century include the following:

- 1919-1922: In Egypt, the Egyptian Revolution was a nonviolent revolution against the British occupation of the country. Egyptians of all types practiced nonviolent resistance, which eventually led to the independence of Egypt in 1922 and the creation of an Egyptian constitution in 1923.
- 1920-1947: The nonviolent resistance movement led by Mahatma Gandhi in India is probably the most famous in history. Thanks to

his views and influence in India, Gandhi was able to bring about the independence of India as well as laws to expand the rights of women and improve the status of the untouchables.

- 1955-1968: Based off Gandhi's methods, the Civil Rights Movement in the United States brought about massive legislative change, making it illegal for African-Americans to be segregated to separate seats, drinking fountains, and schools.
- 1970-1981: In a small example of what nonviolent resistance can do, the people near Larzac, France, led a nonviolent resistance against the expansion of a military base near their farms. After ten years of resistance, the expansion was cancelled.
- 1987-1990: The Singing Revolution was an amazing revolution in which mass demonstrations began with spontaneous singing. With four million singing national songs and hymns that were forbidden by the Soviet Union, which occupied the region, they showed resistance against the ruling government. People would even serve as human shields in front of radio and TV stations to keep Soviet tanks from stopping any coverage of the revolution. This revolution led to the independence of Lithuania, Latvia, and Estonia.
- 1989: The Velvet Revolution in Czechoslovakia involved citizens using passive resistance to earn independence from the Soviet Union. Citizens would paint over street signs to frustrate Russian soldiers. They would cut off water supplies and decorate buildings with flowers and slogans. One of the most popular slogans showed how a small entity could take down something much larger, "An elephant cannot swallow a hedgehog." Eventually, through the passive resistance, Czechoslovakia won its independence from the Soviet Union and was instrumental in taking down the Iron Curtain and ending the Cold War.

Breaking up Big Business

Many will argue that the best way to change the capitalistic system is to break up big business into smaller businesses, and in theory, this can work. If something isn't as large, it is no longer as powerful, but there are some noticeable flaws in this plan.

- How does a small business run a power plant?
- How does a small business run the infrastructure of a railroad?
- How does a small business mine minerals to provide the world with its precious resources?

- How does a small business come up with the millions, or billions, of dollars needed to provide people with the products and the services that they need to live their lives on a day-to-day basis?

As you can see, there are several problems with the concept of just having big businesses broken up into smaller businesses. Another point that can be argued is that big businesses can be bought by the government and then used by the government for the service of the people. Well, that does happen in communist countries, and what happens is the following:

1. A monopoly of resources for the government that allows the government to control nearly everything in a person's life.
2. The disparity of resources allocated to individuals as some get more than others depending on their circumstances.
3. Prices are higher since governments are trying to make a profit and, with the monopoly, can dictate what prices to sell things at.
4. A lowering of productivity as companies are no longer trying to work for a profit and therefore have no need to be innovative.
5. A stagnant economy that hurts nearly everyone but those near the top and those who control the means of production.

So the point can be argued to leave big businesses in place, but even this has its problems because no matter what a small business does, it will not be able to outcompete a large business. This is seen time and time again in the case of Walmart.

Walmart is one of the largest companies on earth. It makes more money than most countries, and its employee base is larger than most armies on earth. This gives the company an immense amount of power. It offers low prices, which are nearly impossible to compete against for small businesses, to customers. Small businesses have no power to force suppliers to sell things to them for less, like Walmart does, so they are not able to compete. Walmart, in addition, has been cited for numerous employee violations and even child labor violations due to its practices. However, because the company is so powerful in the capitalistic system, not even governments can work against it. So by using the free market system, it is impossible for small businesses to compete against big businesses like Walmart.

Even if we break down big business into smaller businesses, those smaller businesses will naturally come back together to form a larger business. This is the natural order of the free market and of capitalism.

NAFTA

Some will argue that it is better to change labor laws and stop NAFTA in order to bring about some sort of change. However, this too is flawed.

Created in 1994, NAFTA (North American Free Trade Agreement) is an agreement that was signed by the governments of the United States, Canada, and Mexico; and it creates a trade bloc in North America, which is the largest in the world. It essentially creates free trade throughout these three countries, which has had good and bad effects. Mexico and Canada have seen employment rise and their economies grow as a result of NAFTA, but in the United States, there have been the loss of many jobs as a result of NAFTA. Employment has grown by fifteen million between 1993 and 2001, but employment in the manufacturing industry only grew by 476,000 during that same period. Between 1994 and 2007, net manufacturing employment in the United States fell by 3.6 million.

So there are those that argue if we repeal NAFTA, then big companies will leave the cheaper markets of Canada and Mexico in order to come back to the United States. This leads to the belief that job losses were not a problem before 1994. However, during the 1980s, unemployment was as high as 10 percent, a level not seen since the Great Depression. In fact, after NAFTA was implemented, unemployment rates in the United States fell to their lowest levels since the early 1960s! Clearly, NAFTA did not rob jobs from the United States, but that is often the excuse given. Jobs were being lost in the United States before NAFTA, and they would still be lost after NAFTA.

The world is too globalized now for the repealing of NAFTA to actually matter in any way to bringing back American jobs.

Even if NAFTA was repealed, more and more machines are doing the menial labor that people used to do. Machines make cars, clothing, shoes, furniture, and pretty much everything that you may use in a given day. Machines do not rest, they do not eat, they do not need health benefits, and they do not need to get paid. No matter what happens with NAFTA, corporations will always look for cheaper ways to do things and that means machines and robots.

Chapter Five

Thinking Differently

The surest way to corrupt a youth is to instruct him to hold in higher esteem those who think alike than those who think differently.

—Friedrich Nietzsche

We have gone over capitalism and communism and seen the problems with both. We have assessed how things can be changed, but what really needs to be done? The most important thing that can be done is to think differently. Thinking differently is important because you are going against the crowd. Thinking differently is all about independent thought because you are deciding to think as an individual.

To change the way you think can be difficult. For example, let us say that you returned to 1850 and met a Southern slave owner. You tell him that the Negro was equal in intelligence with the whites. He may pause to think about it, but when he looks around, he sees African-Americans working in the fields. They don't know how to read or write. They seem inferior to him. He also has some interest in believing they are not equal to whites. He is after all a slave owner. How long did this belief persist in the South? Some still exists today.

In order to think independently, then follow these steps to make it happen:

1. The first thing you have to do is get yourself away from how people think. Throughout our lives, we are told how to think by schools, books, the Internet, television, and movies. If you want to think differently, then you need to find your own independent thought, and that means disconnecting from the sources of conventional thinking.

Some of the greatest thinkers in history came about their independent thoughts by going away from conventional sources to find their own paths. As Robert Frost once said,

> I took the one less traveled by,
> And that has made all the difference.

2. Instead of staying on that well-traveled path, you need to immerse yourself in experiences that will go against the perspective that you currently have. You should find new experiences that can challenge the perception that you currently have. This may mean getting involved with subcultures, going to a foreign culture, or reading a book that you may not have read before. You are attempting to adopt a new train of thought by doing this and by doing that; you become an individual who thinks for themselves.

3. Watch things around you, and understand various processes from a distance. Look at how people interact with each other, determine what different cultures do, and learn about what you can do to develop your own individual thought. By watching the world, you can develop a peace of mind that allows you to practice individual thought.

4. If you keep doing the same thing, using the same sensory inputs, then you should try and change things up a bit. If you go to the same places, talk to the same people, and eat the same food, then mix it up and start going somewhere else, talking to new people, and eating food you would have never eaten before. This can help you create a new understanding of yourself and the world around you. Change things up a bit, and before you know it, you will start thinking for yourself.

5. Practice the ability to distrust the thoughts of others that rely on conventional wisdom. If you assume that truths are just truths, and therefore suspend judgment, you are not thinking for yourself. This does not mean you should become cynical at all, but it does mean that rather than just accepting something as self-evident, you should instead raise questions about it. Perhaps your questions will show that it is indeed the truth that should be accepted, but just maybe, you will learn that there is a new truth, and you can help to wake the world up to it.

The independent thought concept can change the world. One thing it can create, which is very important to this book, is the paradigm shift. This term was first used by Thomas Kuhn in *The Structure of Scientific Revolutions*, which described how there could be a change in basic assumptions within the ruling theory of science. This term represents a change in a fundamental model of events, but it is not restricted to only science. In social science and everything else, it can not only cause many changes, but also truly change how people see their world. Outside of science, there have been several examples of how paradigm shifts have changed the world through changing perceptions in social sciences:

- The Keynesian Revolution represented a major shift in the economic theory of macroeconomics.
- The change in humanity toward being more caring toward the environment and the concept of ecological literacy.
- The change from Keynesianism to Monetarism, which again changed economics and the way that corporations and companies use money.

Work with the Current System

When you think about things differently, you can change the world, and that is what we are attempting here. Yes, the current system does not work that great. There are problems with it, things do not work perfectly, but rather than destroying the current system, it is important to work within the current system. By working within the current system, it is easier to change things because you are not completely upending the system, but you are instead using the system to change it.

This is important because people do not like change. They may not like change, but when change happens gradually, within the present system, they will be able to handle the change better than if there was a sudden change. There are several examples of how social change has happened without most people even knowing it.

- For example, for most of human history, only about 10 percent of the world's population lived within cities. This continued for thousands of years until the days of the Industrial Revolution, and then things began to change without people even knowing it. Today, only two percent of the people in the United States work in agriculture, and 90 percent of people live within urban areas. By 2030, 60 percent of the world's population will live within cities. This is a gradual change that has changed our planet incredibly. However, two hundred years ago, if 90 percent of the people who worked and lived in rural areas decided to move into urban areas, it would cause a significant impact on human civilization. It would be too much change for people to handle. As it is, the move from an agrarian society to an urban society happened gradually; thereby, it changed the system from within.

- Change within the system has come in technology. Business, society, and more have changed thanks to the influx of technology that has hit the world in recent years including e-mail, cell phones, social networks, and more.
- To help people in their lives more, universal education was created, and this changed the system from within by making people more educated. They could ask more questions, and think for themselves more.

To change things properly, you must change them from within. You must think differently of the system that exists now and determine just how you could change it from within rather than upending it from the outside.

Difference between Jobs and Income

When people think of jobs, they think income; and when they think of income, they think of jobs. Most people confuse the two (jobs and income) and assume that they are the same thing. This is a common mistake, but it is something that must be changed. We will address how the problem is not jobs but income after we address what jobs and income truly are.

- Income is the means for consumption and savings that opportunity is gained by a person within a certain time frame, and usually, it is thought of in monetary or money form. Income can be a number of things, including the sum of wages, salaries, profits, interest payments, rents, any type of earnings.
- A job is a regular thing that a person performs that creates value for that person or for society in general. It is how someone contributes to society. It allows an individual and society to meet certain needs. Typically, a person begins a job by volunteering, starting a business, or becoming an employee; and a job can range from one hour in length to an entire lifetime in length. When a person trains for a job, it becomes their profession, and a series of jobs held in a lifetime are seen as a career. The definition of a job does not have to include income.

The big culprit that people say is the problem in today's world is job shortages. However, is this really the problem? Are job shortages really what you need to blame for the problems that the world faces? The problem is not a job shortage, it is lack of income.

Income levels have risen over the years, although the recession of 2009 has caused a slight decrease in the average income levels of a household. In 1989, the median household income was $28,906. However, in 2009, the estimated median household income had gone up to $48,500. But if we adjust it for inflation and put the 1989 figure in 2009 prices, the $28,906 becomes $48,463. Even though you made more, things cost more. So have we really made any headway? Are we really any further ahead? Perhaps people could get better jobs.

Abilities vary between people. Not everyone has the ability to be a rocket scientist or a computer programmer or a doctor or a lawyer. There will always be people who cannot work beyond the simple, less-complex jobs. So there could be enough jobs for everyone, but are there enough good-paying jobs for everyone?

Forty years ago, it was possible to buy a vehicle for a few thousand dollars, you could buy a meal for under $10, and you could pay for a trip to the movies for less than a dollar. Today, prices have skyrocketed on everything, but income has not gone up as much. Therefore, people are not making enough to accommodate their costs, and this is shown in the record-high debt levels that people currently have. Today, people pay more toward their debts than ever before and borrowing more than one has is a common practice.

To understand fully how much people use debt spending, let's look at some facts and figures relating to credit card debt:

- The average credit card debt per household is $15,519
- The total amount of credit cards in circulation is 576.4 million, almost twice the population of the United States.
- The average person has 3.5 credit cards.
- Roughly 4 percent of all Americans are past their sixty-day delinquency rate on their credit cards.
- The U.S. credit card default rate is a staggering 11.17 percent.

Household debt has increased over the years, outpacing both the growth in incomes as well as the growth in inflation. Here is a quick rundown of various years since the 1960s when credit cards began to be used.

- 1966: $360.4 billion
- 1972: $555.4 billion
- 1978: $1.105.4 trillion
- 1984: $1.943.3 trillion
- 1990: $3.595.9 trillion
- 1996: $5.190.4 trillion
- 2002: $8.470.7 trillion
- 2006: $12,817.2 trillion

What makes this astonishing is that between 2002 and 2006, four short years, consumer debt grew by more than it did between 1966 and 1990! Four years of debt growth exceeded twenty-four years of debt growth in the past. That is frightening, but it shows very clearly that there is a problem with a lack of income. People are borrowing more to make their ends meet because they are not making enough to pay for everything. Home prices before the recession were out of control, often rising to three times what a home's value should be.

Before we move further, let's look at 1966 and 2006 to show the immense change in how much things have cost. Keep in mind, the average household income went up $10,000 or 24 percent of an increase. Has everything else kept pace with that?

1966
Average cost of a new house: $14,200.00
Average cost of a gallon of gas: $.32 cents
Average cost of a new car: $2,650.00

2006
Average cost of a new house:	$305,900.00	2,054 percent increase
Average cost of a gallon of gas:	$2.48	675 percent increase
Average cost of a new car:	$28,000.00	956 percent increase

Okay, so the average cost of a home went up 2,054 percent while the average cost of gas and a new car went up 675 percent and 956 percent. Incomes went up 25 percent, but the costs of these items went up far higher, and there we see why there is a lack of income and why so many Americans are currently living deep in debt.

Income through Investment

Since there is a lack of income, how can you make more income? How can you build your income without having to work more? You can do it through investment.

One of the wealthiest CEO in America in 2009 was Larry Ellison. He made a staggering $84.5 million. The thing is he made only $6.1 million in his actual pay. The rest was made up of $78.4 million in stocks and options.

This is what we need to do. We need to follow the same path as Larry Ellison and make more income from investment than straight pay.

Through following this path, we gain the same wealth, and all it takes is putting our money into investments. Another good example is Warren Buffett, who is often cited as either the richest or second richest man on earth. He is worth $47,000,000,000, yep that is right $47 billion, and he got most of it through investments.

This gives us something to think about as we move on to the next chapter.

Chapter Six

The Universal Annuity System

This is the moment when we must build on the wealth that open markets have created, and share its benefits more equitably. Trade has been a cornerstone of our growth and global development. But we will not be able to sustain this growth if it favors the few, and not the many.

—*Barack Obama*

What is the universal annuity system, and how could it change the world. Many are coming to believe that this is the most important and revolutionary concept in the past few decades.

What Is Annuity?

An annuity, in financial theory, is a terminating steam of fixed payments over a certain period of time. Annuities come in many different styles including savings accounts, mortgage payments, insurance payments, and more. Annuity payments are also made in many different ways including weekly, monthly, quarterly, yearly, and more.

One type of annuity is the life annuity, which is an insurance product that is issued by a life insurance company, and they give a person an immediate large lump sum payment if the person receiving the insurance payment has made regular payments over many years.

As with most annuities, the life annuity has two different phases. These phases are as follows:

- The accumulation phase, which is when the money is deposited into the account and accumulated over time.
- The distribution phase, which is when the insurance company makes income payments until the death of the annuitants that are listed within the insurance contract.

There are also different types of annuity, these are:

- Fixed and variable annuities—these are annuities where payments are made for fixed amounts or with a fixed interest rate. Variable annuities pay amounts that vary depending on a number of factors.
- Joint annuities—this is when the payments stop at the death of the annuitant(s).

These concepts are not incredibly important for what we are talking about here, but it is important to go over the concept of annuities for a better understanding of this chapter.

What is being talked about here is an equalization of wealth that is built on the framework that already exists in our world. This is not communism because any attempt to create an equalization of wealth must take into consideration human greed.

Human greed has existed for a very long time and will probably be around for a very long time to come. Humans have a need for self-control and to want things. It is ingrained within our minds, and as we have seen, that is why communism has failed. So creating a system that does not allow greed is doomed to failure because that is not how you tackle greed. Greed is tackled by giving people everything that they need in their lives.

It has to be noted that this change toward equalization of wealth must be done without the use of violence.

In addition, changes toward equalization of wealth must be done on a global scale. It cannot be done on a country scale because the world is far too interconnected these days, and therefore, global change must be done.

The Vision of the Universal Annuity System

The universal annuity system cannot be overseen by anything but the United Nations. The United Nations is one of the most important organizations in history, and it is an international organization that could handle the change that can come when the universal annuity system is implemented.

The United Nations is an international organization that was created in 1945 in the wake of World War II as a way of creating cooperation in international law, international security, economic development, social progress, world peace, and human rights. At this time, there are 192 member states, which make up every single sovereign state on the planet. The offices of the United Nations extend to areas all over the world, and the organization itself is made up of roughly six different suborganizations:

- General Assembly—the group that includes everyone in the United Nations.
- Security Council—responsible for creating resolutions of peace and security and preventing war.
- Economic and Social Council—responsible for assisting in creating international social and economic cooperation as well as development.
- Secretariat—responsible for providing information and facilities needed by the United Nations.
- International Court of Justice—responsible for judicial proceedings.
- United Nations Trusteeship Council—this is currently inactive.

The United Nations also has several important agencies within it that could help with the change toward a universal annuity system. These are the following:

- The World Health Organization
- The World Food Program
- The United Nations Children's Fund

The United Nations is clearly the best organization to implement the universal annuity system. Probably the biggest reason for this is because the nations of the world come together in the United Nations to work together. After all, it was the United Nations that created the Universal Declaration of Human Rights.

For those who do not know of this document, it is one of the most important in human history, and the universal annuity system uses many of the concepts within this document to ensure that everyone gets the help that they need in order to live the lives that they deserve.

Universal Declaration of Human Rights

Article 1

All human beings are born free and equal in dignity and rights. They are endowed with reason and conscience and should act towards one another in a spirit of brotherhood.

Article 2

Everyone is entitled to all the rights and freedoms set forth in this Declaration, without distinction of any kind, such as race, colour, sex, language, religion, political or other opinion, national or social origin, property, birth or other status.

Furthermore, no distinction shall be made on the basis of the political, jurisdictional or international status of the country or territory to which a person belongs, whether it be independent, trust, non-self-governing or under any other limitation of sovereignty.

Article 3

Everyone has the right to life, liberty and security of person.

Article 4

No one shall be held in slavery or servitude; slavery and the slave trade shall be prohibited in all their forms.

Article 5

No one shall be subjected to torture or to cruel, inhuman, or degrading treatment or punishment.

Article 6

Everyone has the right to recognition everywhere as a person before the law.

Article 7

All are equal before the law and are entitled without any discrimination to equal protection of the law. All are entitled to equal protection against any discrimination in violation of this Declaration and against any incitement to such discrimination.

Article 8

Everyone has the right to an effective remedy by the competent national tribunals for acts violating the fundamental rights granted him by the constitution or by law.

Article 9

No one shall be subjected to arbitrary arrest, detention or exile.

Article 10

Everyone is entitled in full equality to a fair and public hearing by an independent and impartial tribunal, in the determination of his rights and obligations and of any criminal charge against him.

Article 11

1. Everyone charged with a penal offence has the right to be presumed innocent until proved guilty according to law in a public trial at which he has had all the guarantees necessary for his defense.
2. No one shall be held guilty of any penal offence on account of any act or omission which did not constitute a penal offence, under national or international law, at the time when it was committed. Nor shall a heavier penalty be imposed than the one that was applicable at the time the penal offence was committed.

Article 12

No one shall be subjected to arbitrary interference with his privacy, family, home or correspondence, nor to attacks upon his honour and reputation. Everyone has the right to the protection of the law against such interference or attacks.

Article 13

1. Everyone has the right to freedom of movement and residence within the borders of each State.
2. Everyone has the right to leave any country, including his own, and to return to his country.

Article 14

1. Everyone has the right to seek and to enjoy in other countries asylum from persecution.
2. This right may not be invoked in the case of prosecutions genuinely arising from non-political crimes or from acts contrary to the purposes and principles of the United Nations.

Article 15

1. Everyone has the right to a nationality.
2. No one shall be arbitrarily deprived of his nationality nor denied the right to change his nationality.

Article 16

1. Men and women of full age, without any limitation due to race, nationality or religion, have the right to marry and to found a family. They are entitled to equal rights as to marriage, during marriage, and at its dissolution.
2. Marriage shall be entered into only with the free and full consent of the intending spouses.
3. The family is the natural and fundamental group unit of society and is entitled to protection by society and the State.

Article 17

1. Everyone has the right to own property alone as well as in association with others.
2. No one shall be arbitrarily deprived of his property.

Article 18

Everyone has the right to freedom of thought, conscience, and religion; this right includes freedom to change his religion or belief, and freedom, either alone or in community with others and in public or private, to manifest his religion or belief in teaching, practice, worship and observance.

Article 19

Everyone has the right to freedom of opinion and expression; this right includes freedom to hold opinions without interference and to seek, receive and impart information and ideas through any media and regardless of frontiers.

Article 20

1. Everyone has the right to freedom of peaceful assembly and association.
2. No one may be compelled to belong to an association.

Article 21

1. Everyone has the right to take part in the government of his country, directly or through freely chosen representatives.
2. Everyone has the right to equal access to public service in his country.
3. The will of the people shall be the basis of the authority of government; this will shall be expressed in periodic and genuine elections which shall be by universal and equal suffrage and shall be held by secret vote or by equivalent free voting procedures.

Article 22

Everyone, as a member of society, has the right to social security and is entitled to realization, through national effort and international co-operation and in accordance with the organization and resources of each State, of the economic, social and cultural rights indispensable for his dignity and the free development of his personality.

Article 23

1. Everyone has the right to work, to free choice of employment, to just and favourable conditions of work and to protection against unemployment.
2. Everyone, without any discrimination, has the right to equal pay for equal work.
3. Everyone who works has the right to just and favourable remuneration ensuring for himself and his family an existence worthy of human dignity, and supplemented, if necessary, by other means of social protection.
4. Everyone has the right to form and to join trade unions for the protection of his interests.

Article 24

Everyone has the right to rest and leisure, including reasonable limitation of working hours and periodic holidays with pay.

Article 25

1. Everyone has the right to a standard of living adequate for the health and well-being of himself and of his family, including food, clothing, housing and medical care and necessary social services, and the right to security in the event of unemployment, sickness, disability, widowhood, old age or other lack of livelihood in circumstances beyond his control.
2. Motherhood and childhood are entitled to special care and assistance. All children, whether born in or out of wedlock, shall enjoy the same social protection.

Article 26

1. Everyone has the right to education. Education shall be free, at least in the elementary and fundamental stages. Elementary education shall be compulsory. Technical and professional education shall be made generally available and higher education shall be equally accessible to all on the basis of merit.
2. Education shall be directed to the full development of the human personality and to the strengthening of respect for human rights and fundamental freedoms. It shall promote understanding, tolerance and friendship among all nations, racial or religious groups, and shall further the activities of the United Nations for the maintenance of peace.
3. Parents have a prior right to choose the kind of education that shall be given to their children.

Article 27

1. Everyone has the right freely to participate in the cultural life of the community, to enjoy the arts and to share in scientific advancement and its benefits.
2. Everyone has the right to the protection of the moral and material interests resulting from any scientific, literary or artistic production of which he is the author.

Article 28

Everyone is entitled to a social and international order in which the rights and freedoms set forth in this Declaration can be fully realized.

Article 29

1. Everyone has duties to the community in which alone the free and full development of his personality is possible.
2. In the exercise of his rights and freedoms, everyone shall be subject only to such limitations as are determined by law solely for the purpose of securing due recognition and respect for the rights and freedoms of others and of

meeting the just requirements of morality, public order and the general welfare in a democratic society.

3. These rights and freedoms may in no case be exercised contrary to the purposes and principles of the United Nations.

Article 30

Nothing in this Declaration may be interpreted as implying for any State, group or person any right to engage in any activity or to perform any act aimed at the destruction of any of the rights and freedoms set forth herein.

The United Nations has shown that it is an organization that has the ability to eliminate diseases, provide famine relief, do worldwide census takings, help the environment, and jump many hurdles that other organizations have not been able to. With this history behind it, it is clear that the United Nations could easily help bring the universal annuity system into being better than any other organization.

So how would it work? Each nation on earth would be expected to contribute a certain amount every year into a fund that would be used to invest in. The fund would essentially act as a pension fund and those who could collect on the pension fund would be everyone on the entire planet.

Here is a simplistic example to help you understand:

Let us say there are eight billion people in the world. If the fund had $160 billion in it and if the fund made 5 percent return, then each person would receive one dollar in annuities every year. Not much for now, but remember, each nation is contributing to the fund and the fund will increase each year. When the fund has $1.6 trillion in it with 5 percent return, then everyone will receive $10 in annuities. This may not have much effect in the United States, but in other countries, the money would be useful. At $16 trillion and 5 percent returns, everyone will receive $100 in annuities. And so forth on up until we reach a level we wish to stop at, if any. If we were making $10,000 or more a year in annuities, the effect on the economy would be enormous.

Amount in Fund	Individual Payment
• $160 billon	$1.00
• $1.6 trillion	$10.00
• $16 trillion	$100.00
• $160 trillion	$1000.00
• $1.6 quadrillion	$10,000.00

Another example, there are close to seven billion people on the entire planet and if all the member states of the United Nations put in $1 billion (a small amount) into the fund each year, that would create $192 billion in the fund. If the fund received 5 percent of a rate of return each year, then the amount each person would get would break down to the following. Each year, all the money is paid out to citizens of the earth, countries put in $192,000,000,000 and the 5 percent rate of return earned stays in the fund so it could be depicted in this way: Country Contributions + Amount Earned from Rate of Returns.

Amount in Fund	*Individual Payment*
• $192,000,000,000	$27.43
• $201,600,000,000	$28.80
• $211,680,000,000	$30.24
• $222,264,000,000	$31.75
• $233,377,200,000	$33.34
• $245,046,060,000	$35.01
• $257,298,363,000	$36.76

This is just by putting $1 billion in each year from every country in the United Nations. If countries put in $10 billion every year, then people would be paid hundreds of dollars every single year. While many may think that is a lot of money, when you look at other things countries spend money on, it really isn't. Here are the largest defense budgets within NATO:

1.	United States of America	$667.7 billion
2.	United Kingdom	$57.67 billion
3.	France	$54.60 billion
4.	Germany	$38.15 billion
5.	Italy	$33.45 billion
6.	Canada	$18.29 billion
7.	Spain	$14.30 billion
8.	Turkey	$11.59 billion
9.	Netherlands	$10.23 billion
10.	Greece	$7.323 billion

So the United States could actually pay for every country on earth into the fund and still have much more money than any other country on earth in terms of its defense budget. So clearly, there is money that can be spent into the budget without taking money away from anything important. In fact, if each of the top ten countries put in 25 percent of their defense budget into the universal annuity fund, each country would give the following:

1. United States of America $166.93 billion
2. United Kingdom $14.42 billion
3. France $13.65 billion
4. Germany $9.54 billion
5. Italy $8.36 billion
6. Canada $4.57 billion
7. Spain $3.58 billion
8. Turkey $2.90 billion
9. Netherlands $2.56 billion
10. Greece $1.83 billion

How much does this come to in total? If we add up 25 percent of the defense budget of the ten countries on earth with the largest defense budgets, we get the following: $228,340,000,000.

As we can see, by taking just the ten largest military budgets within NATO and taking 25 percent of those budgets, we come to more than the universal annuity fund would make in its first four years of 5 percent rate of return and every country putting in a total of $192 billion. That is not too bad.

Clearly, there is money on the planet that can be used; it is just about getting countries to start using it in the right way.

Hope Equity

Could an investment give a return that can help people? There is a model of just such a process. The nonprofit company called Hope Equity is just such a business. It takes donations and invests them. They then take a portion of return from their investment and distribute it to your chosen cause. Some part of the returns is put back in the original account and the account grows over time. Currently, the portion of the returns is about 5.5 percent.

Chapter Seven

Difficulties with the System

Every great man, every successful man, no matter what the field of endeavor, has known the magic that lies in these words: every adversity has the seed of an equivalent or greater benefit.

—*W. Clement Stone*

I would like to say that the universal annuity system can be created without any problems. That it can begin to work with a smooth transition but this is just not the case. There are going to be some difficulties to start off with, but those difficulties must be overcome for the greater good and for the creation and preservation of the UAS. Adversity and difficulties are normal, and this does not mean that the UAS is doomed to fail. In fact, it will make it stronger because by conquering adversity, it is possible to grow from it and learn from it.

The Amount of Money

Probably the most glaring problem comes from the fact that a large amount of money is needed. As we have stated, if $192 billion is to be used, then $1 billion from every country needs to be rounded up. However, even more money will be needed to make a big difference in individual lives, and that requires countries putting in at least $10 billion each to bring it up to $1.92 trillion. That is an immense amount of money, but it is possible, and it just requires that some things be put together to make it easier to deal with the large amount of money.

To deal with the large amount of money needed, the best thing to do is to reduce the number of people that would get the money. So we would set a minimum age limit of seventy, and as time goes on, that could be reduced. So the minimum age will come down over time to include those in their sixties, fifties, and so on down to any point you want to stop. What kind of effect would this have? This would take hundreds of millions of people out of the equation, and as a result, not as much money would be needed. Instead of needing to contribute $10 billion each to make a difference, countries may only need to contribute roughly $5 billion as a result. The UAS could start out as a supplemental pension plan. The eventual point of the universal annuity system is to help those out who are of working age and the young who will one day be working. It will give them a leg up.

Corruption

Corruption is a very serious problem around the world, and there is the risk of fraud with the sheer amount of money that is being deposited. People would be receiving money each year for a few hundred dollars each, and if a government wanted to or officers in the government wanted to, they could take the money for themselves. If a government has a population of thirty million people and they take half of the money for themselves and each check is for $300, that would give the government $4.5 billion! That is too much for some countries to resist, and that means there is a great deal of corruption potential. What countries are the most likely and least likely to rob their own citizens? We have to look to the United Nations Corruption Perceptions Index for that.

Least Corrupt

These countries are the least likely to rob their own citizens and therefore are most likely to provide the money from the universal annuity system to the people in the country: New Zealand, Denmark, Singapore, Sweden, Switzerland, Finland, Netherlands, Australia, Canada, Iceland, Norway, Hong Kong, Luxembourg, Germany, Ireland, Austria, Japan, United Kingdom, United States, Barbados, Belgium, Qatar, Saint Lucia, France, and Chile

Most Corrupt

These countries represent the biggest risk for stealing from their citizens and robbing them of the benefit of the universal annuity system: Somalia,

Afghanistan, Myanmar, Sudan, Iraq, Chad, Uzbekistan, Turkistan, Iran, Haiti, Guinea, Equatorial Guinea, Burundi, Venezuela, Kyrgyzstan, Guinea-Bissau, Democratic Republic of the Congo, Angola, Tajikistan, Laos, Central African Republic, Cambodia, Yemen, Paraguay, and Papua New Guinea.

These countries will most likely rob their citizens. So how do you fix this? Well, first of all, there should be direct deposit into banking accounts for people because the sheer volume of checks each year would be too much. There would be seven billion checks going out and that is physically expensive. A direct deposit method would be best with little cost. To do this of course, the country would need to have a good banking system. Some type of requirements would be needed to join the universal annuity system.

Requirements

The United Nations would need to put together something along the lines of what the European Union requires for its members. There can be a series of criteria for a country to qualify for the universal annuity system just as there are criteria that the European Union has for its member country applications. To give a better understanding of what would be required, here is a rundown of the requirement of what the European Union requires. Obviously, the most important criteria is the fact that the country must be on the European landmass, but the rest of the criteria can be applied to the universal annuity system.

- The government must be a democracy that allows all citizens to be able to participate on an equal basis through political decision making on every level of government. This means free elections with a secret ballot, the right to start a political party, free press, and free trade unions.
- Government authority can only be exercised within the country in accordance with documented laws and established procedures.
- Every person in the country must have the basic human rights extended to them including the right to life, the right to be prosecuted only in accordance with the laws in existence at the time, the right to be free from slavery, and the right to be free from the threat of torture.
- Minorities within the country must be allowed to retain their cultural practices, including their language, without suffering discrimination.
- All member countries must have a functioning market economy that has the ability to cope with competitive pressure and market forces within the union.

So these same principles could be applied to countries wishing to join in on the universal annuity system. Other criteria could include a well-established banking system, an accurate census system, and other criteria. While this may eliminate a lot of countries, it would allow some of the largest economies on earth to take part. The European Union, Canada, United States, Australia, and Japan could all take part immediately, and they make up a huge portion of the wealth of the world.

Investment Companies

The UAS would be run by a committee of the UN, but they would not do the investing themselves. What should be done is thousands of investment companies should handle the investing for the UN so the UN will only need to do three things:

1. Watch the fund for its progress.
2. Distribute the money from the fund into hands of its citizens.
3. Set up the criteria for each government to join.

Equal Distribution

There will be a desire to distribute the return on investments on an unequal basis. It will seem unjust to give, say, Donald Trump a hundred dollars for a cigar and someone else a hundred dollars to buy milk and bread. If we do not give everyone the same amount of money then we will be needing a large bureaucracy to sort things out. But we already have a large bureaucracy to sort things out. It is called the IRS. Let's not duplicate bureaucracy.

Chapter Eight

Benefits of the Universal Annuity System

We think sometimes that poverty is only being hungry, naked, and homeless. The poverty of being unwanted, unloved, and uncared for is the greatest poverty. We must start in our own homes to remedy this kind of poverty.

—*Mother Teresa*

There are several benefits to the universal annuity system, which may seem pretty clear at first. The fact that people will get money that they need to live the lives they want for one. However, there are some other benefits to the universal annuity system that you may not realize. In this chapter, we will focus on the things that the universal annuity system can do for the world and how it can help the world go into the future.

Elimination of Extreme Poverty

Extreme poverty is a serious problem around the world, and while the fewest amounts of people in history currently live in extreme poverty than at any time in history, there are still millions who go without on a grand scale.

What is extreme poverty exactly? Extreme poverty is the most severe form of poverty in which people cannot meet their basic human needs of food, water, shelter, sanitation, and health care.

According to the World Bank, *extreme poverty* is defined as "anyone who is making less than $1.25 per day." Yes, that is right, per day. Currently, 1.4

billion people on the planet live under these conditions. Naturally, this is a serious problem and the United Nations made the elimination of extreme hunger and poverty the number one Millennium Development Goal set in 2000. The most common areas of extreme poverty are sub-Saharan Africa and South Asia, and most experts feel that diseases like AIDS, malaria, and tuberculosis in these countries are big factors in and consequences from extreme poverty.

That all being said, the number of people who live in poverty has gone down immensely, from 59 percent in 1981 to only 19 percent today. That is a drop of 40 percent and the universal annuity system can help eliminate the problems of extreme poverty through this innovative system.

With the UAS, extreme poverty would be eliminated because if everyone got $457 per year as part of the system, then all those people who only make $1.25 per day would suddenly have a year's worth of salary added to what they already made. That would double their income and push them up to making $2.50 per day. While that is not immense, it is a start, and as time goes on, more and more people will come out of extreme poverty.

Better Tax Base

When countries have citizens who make more money, they get the added benefit that they now have more citizens paying money in taxes. More money in taxes allows a country to spend more money on such things as the following:

1. Better roads and infrastructure that would allow people and business to travel freely throughout the country.
2. Better health services, which then gives people the ability to live longer lives and better lives free of many curable diseases.
3. Better protection services like fire and police. This then helps make countries safer thereby reducing the threat of warlords, murders, rapes, thefts, assaults, and more. A safer country also receives more tourism, which brings more money into the country as a whole.
4. Better educational systems. This is very important because when education levels go up, that means people will learn more and question more. This leads people to want things like democracy and equal rights, and it can be a big force of change in a country that usually resists it.

No Social Security, Retirement Plans, Welfare

Many critics of social systems feel that they take money away from people who want to work. If we follow the concept of the UAS to a higher level, there would be no need for social security or retirement plans or welfare.

Criminals Pay Their Way

Across the planet, there are about ten million people that are imprisoned for various offenses. Imprisoning a person costs a lot of money for a government. Under the universal annuity system, there would be no need to pay for criminals to be in jail. Criminals would be earning money from the universal annuity system and they could pay their own way. This would help save governments a lot of money that they could use to fighting crime at its root by giving people the ability to live the lives they desire, rather than forcing them into crime as a necessity.

Crime itself would decrease. There would be less motivation for crime if people had a basic income. There would also be the disincentive to commit crime if you know that you would be paying for your own incarceration.

More Interest in the Economy

One of the more interesting benefits from the universal annuity system is that people will have more economic interest in the economy. They will be making money from the economic structure. As a result, they will be less likely to want to destroy it. The citizens of the world will not want the economy destroyed. Support for terrorist groups such as al-Qaeda will be reduced.

Chapter Nine

The Future of Work

All labor that uplifts humanity has dignity and importance and should be undertaken with painstaking excellence.

—Martin Luther King, Jr.

There will be many changes in the world when the universal annuity system is implemented. They come from the fact that people will then have the money to live the way they want and governments will have the money to implement important things like health care, education, and infrastructure. So what kinds of other types of changes will be seen in the world when the UAS is well established?

Robots

Robots already make cars, do a lot of assembly line work, and the technology exists today for more robots to be used in many different types of work. With robots being used to do less desirable work, that will free people up to do more of what they enjoy and to pursue their own dreams.

Some things that robots could easily do now with today's technology include the following:

- Building cars
- Building products on an assembly line
- Cleaning
- Making food in fast food environments

- Janitorial services
- Protection
- Maintenance

There are literally thousands of jobs that robots can do, and if robots do that work, there are other benefits. The biggest benefit is the low production costs to make things that robots make. Robots do not have to be paid, they do not take breaks, they work 24-7, they do not need health care, and they can work faster than any human can. This means that goods can be made for roughly 25 percent of what goods made by humans can make. When goods are cheaper to make, they are cheaper to buy.

Laziness

With people having everything they need because of more money coming to them and cheaper goods thanks to production by robots, there is the risk of laziness. When people win the lottery, they will sometimes quit their job and stop doing things. Well, there is the risk that people will become lazy and not want to do anything. The number of couch potatoes may increase but something else will happen; more people will do what they want. The rich have enough money to retire on, but they continue to work because they are doing something that they love. It is the same if everyone has everything that they need. There will be an increase in the number of artists, collectors, and inventors.

It is easy to say that when you have enough money, you will not do any work. Many people will find that boring very quickly. There are those that retire but find they need to do something. Many retirees volunteer, work odd jobs, or work at Walmart or McDonalds.

You may begin to look at what you would do in your life. You will look at what you can do that will keep your interest and make you want to get out of bed in the morning. People in these circumstances could ask themselves these questions:

1. I have all that I need, what do I enjoy doing?
2. Do the things I enjoy doing qualify as a job that I can do?
3. What can I do that will benefit humanity the most?
4. What can I do that not necessarily pays the most, but will make me the happiest?

At that point, people will begin to get into the careers that they want to get into because that is what interests them. As a result, they will be helping humanity because they are helping themselves. There is an adage that says when you better yourself, you better the human race, and that is exactly what would happen here. Do you want a doctor that is in it for the money or one that is a doctor because he wants to help people?

The Meaning of Money

If you follow the concept of the UAS, perhaps money will become meaningless. If money becomes meaningless what type of world will we live in? Perhaps one in line with the future vision such as *Star Trek*, where exploration and the pursuit of knowledge is the most important things in the universe.

In Conclusion

It is incumbent on man to perpetuate a just and equitable economic system. Though some have sought their own advantage, there persists a constant vein of justice that runs through the body of man's civilization. It ever pushes mankind forward. With fits and starts and times at which it appears that man's destiny was to destroy itself, it never evaporated completely. In the end, civilization is ever advancing. In that pursuit, he is ever evaluating and reevaluating his government, his laws, his society, his heart, his mind, and thus, his whole being. One aspiration that has slipped through man's groping fingers has been the equal distribution of wealth, the justice in economics, the foundation of every perfect utopia. Through the ages, man's imagination has dwelled on this problem. From Plato to Thomas More to Karl Marx, the thoughts of man have envisioned this hope. Many imaginative stories have been developed to entertain the human mind. The possible existence of such fantasies becomes impossible in the tangible world.

The universal annuity system has the potential to change the world and bring about large social change. It is not done through violence, it is not communism, and it is a new form of capitalism. It allows things to stay the way they are in some sense because the real change will come from the people who suddenly realize that they have everything they need to survive. They will begin to make the changes to make the world a better place, and it all begins with the universal annuity system.

www.ingramcontent.com/pod-product-compliance
Lightning Source LLC
Chambersburg PA
CBHW021912170526
45157CB00005B/2054